Orchids
Coloring Book

Mother Nature Series

Author Artist   Jeri Lee C.Ht.

ISBN: 9798379204525

This Book
Belongs To
Name

ORCHIDS

Orchids are one of the largest and most diverse families of flowering plants, with over 25,000 species found in nearly every part of the world. The name "orchid" is derived from the Greek word for testicles because of their unique bulbous shape. Orchids have a reputation for being difficult to grow, but they can be quite easy if you provide them with the right conditions and care for them properly. Orchids come in a wide variety of colors, including white, pink, yellow, purple, and even near-black varieties like Dracula orchids! Some orchids produce fragrant blooms that smell like vanilla or chocolate, while others don't produce any scent at all! In some cultures, orchids symbolize fertility and good luck. In contrast, in other cultures, they represent luxury and beauty due to their intricate designs and delicate petals, which make them highly sought after by collectors worldwide! . There are many different types of orchid species that can be grown indoors as houseplants, such as phalaenopsis (moth) orchid and cymbidiums (boat) orchid, which both require bright indirect light to thrive inside your home environment! Orchids are often used in floral arrangements due to their long-lasting flowers, which typically last up to three months when appropriately kept hydrated – making them perfect for special occasions like weddings!

Mother Earth Series

Welcome to my Mother Earth Series of Coloring Books! This series was created to inspire respect for our planet and its many families of life. It focuses on the beauty, harmony, and balance of nature that is so essential to sustaining life on earth. Through these books, we hope to bring awareness of how important it is for us all to work together in protecting our environment and creating a better future for generations to come. The Mother Earth series explores the delicate relationship between humans and nature by featuring stunning artwork depicting The birds, Bees, Butterflies and plants. Animals, both on land and at sea I feature in my series Save the Planet. Please check them out and more. Each page encourages interaction with vibrant colors while providing an opportunity for reflection on our impact upon this beautiful world we call home. The message behind each book is simple: Respect Nature! We can make a difference in preserving our planet if we choose eco-friendly solutions when possible such as using reusable items instead of disposable ones; conserving energy through efficient lighting; eating organic food grown without harmful chemicals; reducing water waste; recycling materials whenever possible; supporting renewable energy sources like solar or wind power; avoiding single-use plastics whenever you can — just some examples from what could be done every day in order to protect our environment. We are living beings within a complex web of interconnectedness that includes plants, animals (including ourselves), air quality, water resources – even climate change -all intricately linked together. We owe it not only ourselves but also future generations who will inherit this magnificent world that has been entrusted into our care today—to recognize its importance and use wisdom when choosing actions which affect the environment around us now & forevermore! Thank you for joining us as part of this journey towards a sustainable future – one coloring book at a time! If you enjoy my work, plesase leave me a positive review.

Thank You For Purchasing my Book

If you enjoyed it

Please give me a good review

Save the Planet Series

If you enjoy my books please give me a Positive review.

these and Many More

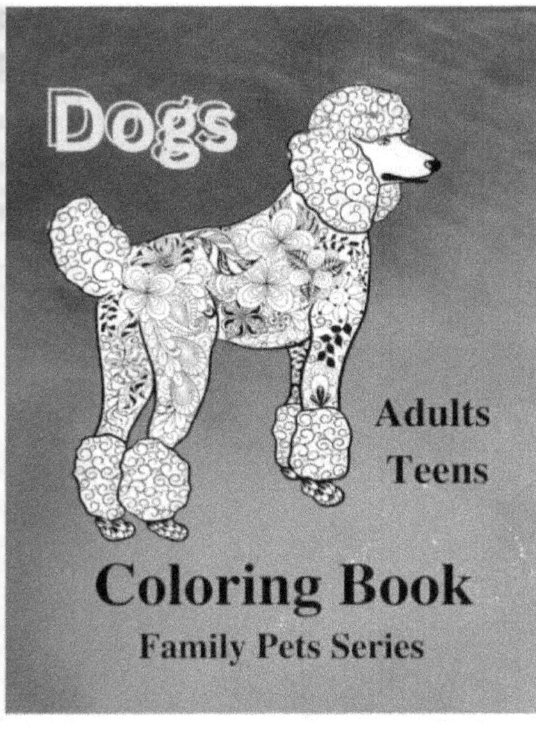

Many
MORE

More Pet Books you might Enjoy

UNIVERSAL

PEACE

www.ingramcontent.com/pod-product-compliance
Lightning Source LLC
Chambersburg PA
CBHW081650260726
48653CB00009BA/3413